THE AMAZING HUMAN BODY

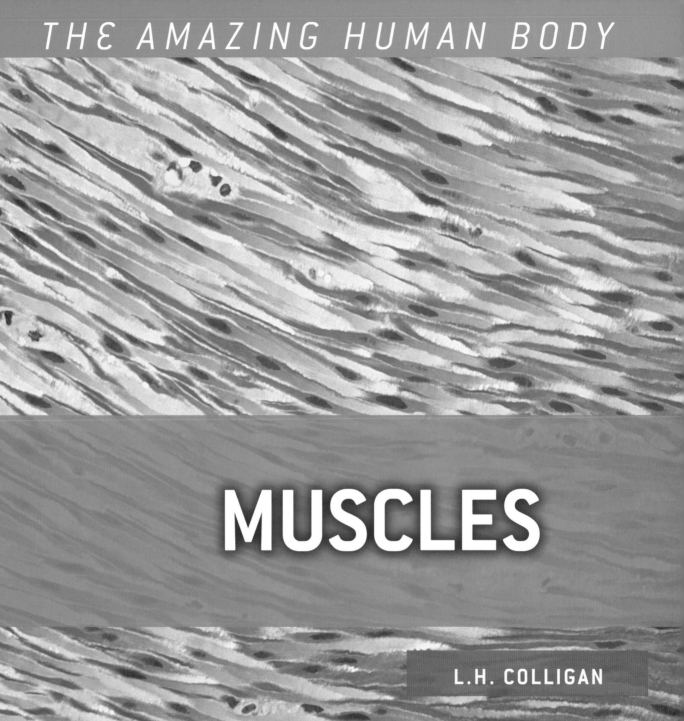

MUSCLES

L.H. COLLIGAN

Marshall Cavendish
Benchmark

Marshall Cavendish Benchmark
99 White Plains Road
Tarrytown, New York 10591
www.marshallcavendish.us

Editor: Karen Ang
Publisher: Michelle Bisson
Art Director: Anahid Hamparian
Series Design by Kay Petronio
Series Designer: Elynn Cohen

Library of Congress Cataloging-in-Publication Data
Colligan, L. H.
 Muscles / by L.H. Colligan.
   p. cm. -- (The amazing human body)
 Includes bibliographical references and index.
 Summary: "Discusses human musculature, what can go wrong, how to treat those diseases and injuries, and
how to stay healthy"--Provided by publisher.
 ISBN 978-0-7614-4038-3
 1. Muscles--Juvenile literature. I. Title.
 QP321.C725 2010
 612.7'4--dc22
 2008037257

This book is not intended for use as a substitute for advice, consultation, or treatment by a licensed medical practitioner. The
reader is advised that no action of a medical nature should be taken without consultation with a licensed medical practitioner,
including action that may seem to be indicated by the contents of this work, since individual circumstances vary and medical
standards, knowledge, and practices change with time. The publisher, author, and medical consultants disclaim all liability
and cannot be held responsible for any problems that may arise from use of this book.

Front cover image: Human muscles
Title page: Smooth muscle fibers
Back cover: Skeletal muscle fibers

 = skeletal muscle

Photo research by Tracey Engel

Front cover photo: Douglas R. Hess / Shutterstock .
The photographs in this book are used by permission and through the courtesy of:
Getty Images: Spike Walker, 1; Dr. Dennis Kunkel / Visuals Unlimited, Inc., back cover, 13; Dr. Fred Hossler, 4; Michael Najjar, 8;
3D4 Medical.com, 9, 28, 29, 35, 50; Dr. Richard Kessel & Dr. Randy Kardon/Tissues & Organs, 11, 33; Sean Justice, 15, 57; Dorling
Kindersly, 17; Britt Erlanson, 18; Dr. David Phillips, 20; DEA Picture Library, 24; Biodisc, 26, 45; Dr. David M. Phillips, 34; Hulton
Archive, 43; Reuben Paris, 52; Lisa Spindler Photography Inc., 58; Patryce Bak, 62; Alexander Hubrich, 67; Chris Garrett, 69. Photo
Researches, Inc.: Anatomical Travelogue, 6; SPL, 12; CMEABG-UCBL-CHAPON / PHANIE, 38; PHANIE, 40; Roger J. Bick & Brian J.
Poindexter / UT-Houston Medical School, 41 (left and right); Alix, 47; Patrick Landmann, 48; Lea Paterson, 49; Dr. P. Marazzi, 54,
55; Living Art Enterprises, 64; Mark Turnball, 65. Alamy: Nucleus Medical Art, Inc., 23, 25, 46; Dr. Dennis Kunkel Microscopy Inc. /
PHOTOTAKE, 36; First Light, 42; imagebroker, 53; Bob Jones Photography, 60; mediablitzimages (uk) Limited, 56; B2M Productions,
68. Shutterstock: Patrick Hermans, 7. SuperStock: Image Source, 10. Corbis: LWA-Stephen Welstead, 66. .

Printed in Malaysia
123456

CONTENTS

1

What Are Muscles?

The muscles in the human body can be divided into three main networks of specialized muscle tissues. These networks move our bones, blood vessels, internal organs, and more, twenty-four hours a day. Within the three systems, more than eight hundred muscles generate movement and heat when they contract—or tighten—during use, or relax when not in use.

The three main muscle systems are the skeletal muscle system, the smooth muscle system, and the cardiac muscle system. The skeletal muscle system holds our bones in place so that we remain upright. This voluntary system responds when we tell our bodies to use muscles to do things like clench a fist or run. The smooth muscle system lines many

Different types of muscle fibers are responsible for many voluntary and involuntary actions in the body.

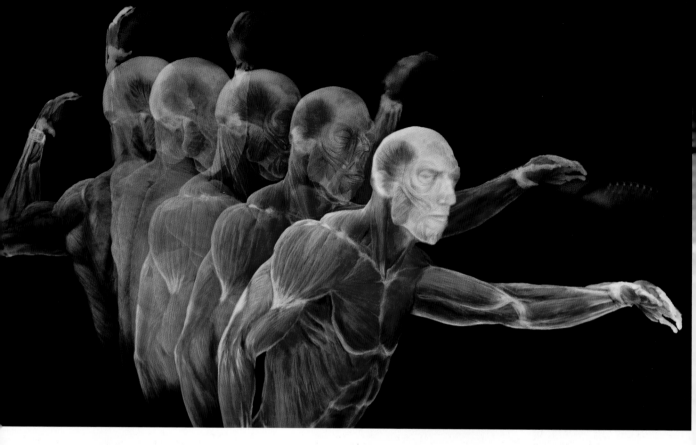

The seemingly simple act of throwing something is actually a complex process that involves the muscles and other body systems, such as the nervous and skeletal systems.

internal organs, such as the liver and kidneys. It helps to push substances, such as blood, food, and waste, through the body. The cardiac muscle system helps the heart pump blood throughout the body. We cannot tell the smooth or cardiac muscle systems what to do. These two involuntary systems work automatically.

Muscles give us the power to smile, frown, speak, chew, jump, climb, throw a ball, type, digest the food we eat, read these words, and much more. With all these jobs, it is no wonder that muscles in the three muscle systems make up the highest percentage of body weight in an average-sized person. That is more than the weights of bones, fat, blood, or other tissues.

When healthy muscles are well fed, exercised, and rested, they can literally make us jump for joy. The flexibility and support muscles provide make it possible for us to participate in life.

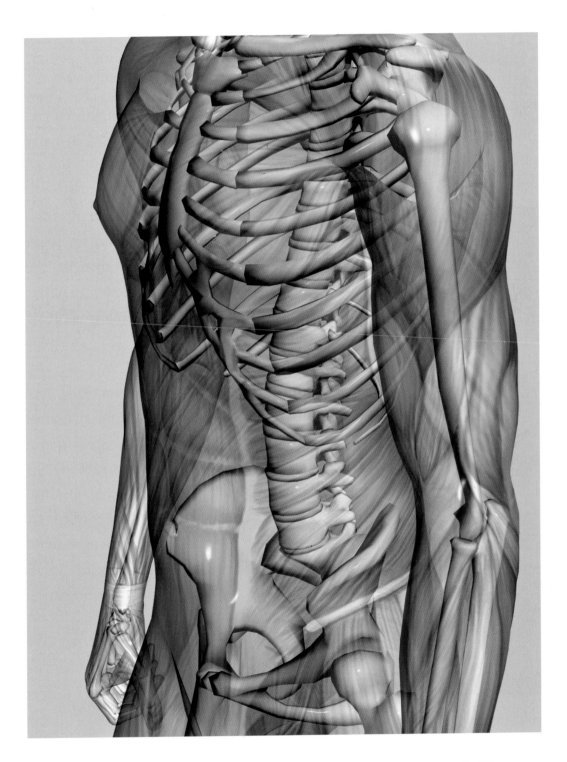

Muscles are found throughout the body and help to protect organs and other parts, all while allowing us to move and balance.

WHAT MUSCLES DO

Muscles perform several major jobs. They take energy from nutrients in the food we eat and use it to move our bodies. Muscles work in pairs to create movement. When one muscle contracts, the muscle it is paired with relaxes.

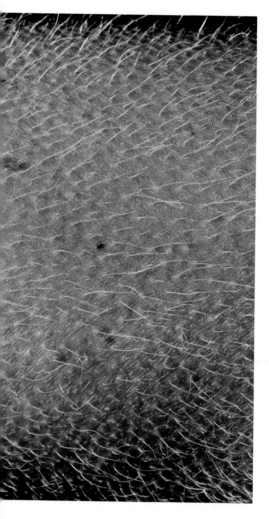

Healthy muscles maintain muscle tone—or structure—because they are always somewhat tightened. Muscle tone means that muscles are working, keeping us upright and ready to move. Even during sleep, muscles remain slightly contracted.

Muscles help to keep our body healthy. Muscle contractions create heat and keep the body at its ideal temperature. If cold air starts to lower body temperature, tiny muscles—goose bumps at the base of each hair—contract to hold in body heat. When outside conditions are hot, these same tiny muscles expand to let out heat and cool us down. Healthy muscles also provide a layer of protective tissues over organs, such as the liver and kidneys, and other structures inside the body.

Goose bumps are the result of tiny muscles tightening and making fine body hairs stand up.

MUSCLE STRUCTURE

The organization of muscle structures makes them strong. Imagine layers of stretchy cylinders inside other stretchy cylinders then stacked into bundles. Such bundles would resemble muscles. They are packed, multi-layered, and hard, yet flexible.

Even the largest, firmest muscle on a body builder is made up of delicate threadlike structures called muscle fibers. These fibers are actually cells, the smallest basic unit in an organism. Under a microscope, a single muscle cell, or fiber, looks thin and fragile. Yet each fiber is packed with many filaments. Myofibril filaments are

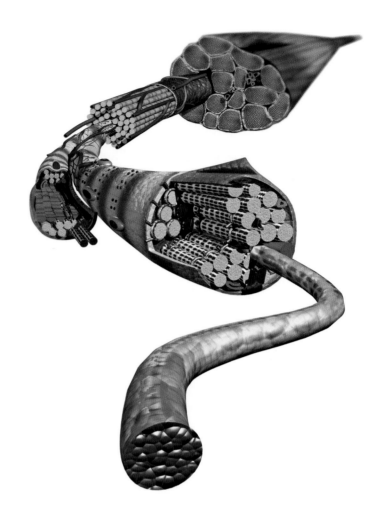

Muscles are made up of smaller fibers, which give them great strength and flexibility.

coated cylinders. Within them are thick and thin myofilaments. The thicker ones are made of a chemical protein substance called actin. The thin myofilaments contain myosin proteins. Groups of myofilament cylinders are bundled into units called sarcomeres. Inside sarcomeres, actin and myosin proteins, slide past each other. This sliding makes muscles move.

It is hard to imagine that tiny muscle fibers could possibly contain even more structures, but they do. Muscle spindles inside muscle fibers react to muscle stretching. They send messages to the brain that one muscle is stretched out. The brain then causes electrical and chemical changes to relax the paired muscle.

Muscle spindles also communicate with the brain about where muscles are located. They tell the brain things like how an arm is bent or if a leg is up or down. The brain then adjusts the movements of other body parts for balance. Even if you close your eyes, muscle spindles and the brain's messengers (called neurons) work together to tell you your position.

All muscle fiber structures are individually coated with connective tissue, mainly made up of collagen. This natural protein substance strengthens everything it encloses. Bundles of filaments, which are called the fascicles, are also covered with connective tissue. These wrapped, coated bundles form the muscle itself and make each one incredibly strong.

Muscles do not just float around loosely inside the body. Cord-like connective tissues called tendons attach skeletal muscles to bones, skin, or to other muscles. Muscles are also threaded with networks of tiny blood vessels called capillaries and tubules. These carry nutrients and oxygen in blood into the muscles. When muscles are being used, they release chemicals that cause the heart to direct more blood to the muscles from

Collagen can be found in different parts of the body. This connective tissue strengthens muscles.

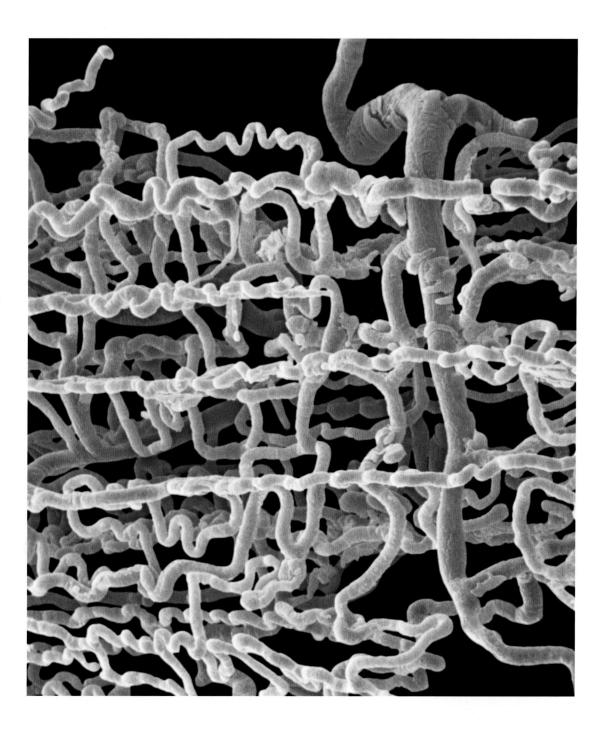

The pink and red tubes shown here are capillaries found in muscles. The blood vessels' many loops and bends allow them to adjust in size and length as the muscles contract and expand.

the other parts of the body. This extra blood gives the muscles an extra boost of oxygen and nutrients so they can move faster and longer.

MUSCLE CHEMISTRY

Living muscles are like laboratories where quick, chemical reactions make energy. Mitochondria, which are microscopic structures inside cells, produce the chemical adenosine triphosphate (ATP). ATP is the major chemical that produces the energy muscles need to move. However, muscle fibers only have a small amount of available ATP. They must get ATP more to keep moving.

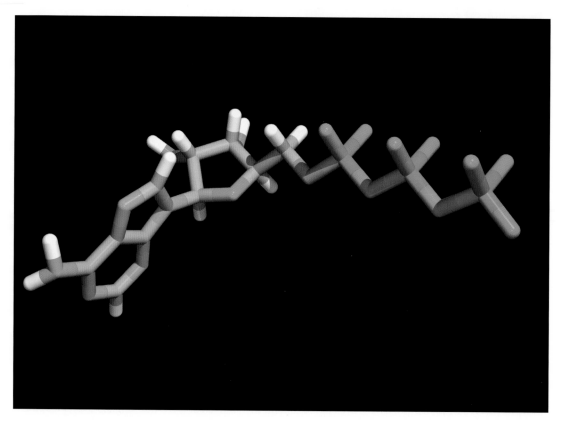

This is the molecular structure of ATP. The human body stores and uses ATP to create the energy needed for everyday life-sustaining activities.

When muscles use up stored ATP, the body breathes harder to take in more oxygen. The heart pumps faster to send more oxygenated blood to muscle cells to make more ATP. Increased oxygen in the blood stimulates the liver to convert glucose sugars from nutrients in food. The liver then releases the glucose into muscle cells, which builds up the ATP levels. With more ATP, thick myofilaments can detach themselves from thin myofilaments so that they can move.

Another chemical reaction begins when electrical signals from the brain cause the release of acetylcholine. This neurotransmitter triggers electrical activity in muscle cells. The cells release stored calcium ions. In turn, calcium makes it possible for thin and thick muscle filaments to slide past each other. When that happens, muscles move.

Chemical reactions in the muscles allow the different-sized filaments and fibers to move.

FIGHT OR FLIGHT?

A car races out of a driveway inches in front of you, or something crashes in another room while you are home alone. In an instant, your heart pounds, your neck prickles, and you breathe harder. You may get goosebumps.

These physical reactions, which happen automatically, are a reaction to danger. In humans and many other organisms, muscles undergo immediate changes. These begin after the brain floods the body with dozens of emergency chemicals, called hormones, which set off a chain reaction of muscle activities.

When certain hormones are released, heart muscles pump more oxygenated blood to muscles in the arms and legs. These muscles tighten to gather energy that may be needed to fly from the danger or fight it directly. Capillaries in the skin constrict so that blood will go to the muscles instead of the skin. The loss of blood near the skin causes chills and goose bumps in scary or stressful situations.

Eye muscles expand. As a result, widened pupils take in more light so that you can see better. Muscles near the lungs relax to let in more oxygen so that breathing speeds up. At the same time, digestive muscles slow down. This increases energy and blood flow to the muscles needed in an emergency. The flight or fight response is an instinct that helps all animals, including humans, to survive dangerous situations.

These are very complicated steps, yet they take place in split seconds. Muscle chemistry also causes cells to convert nutrients into lactic acid. Experts once believed that lactic acid was a waste product that caused in muscle soreness. However, in 2006, scientists discovered that lactic acid is actually a fuel. Hard-working muscles produce lactic acid from glucose. This process gives muscles energy. The muscles of well-trained athletes are particularly efficient at converting lactic acid into energy.

BRAIN AND MUSCLE POWER

Muscles do not work by themselves. They depend on the brain's neurons to tell muscles what to do. For example, if you want to move your little finger, a chain of electrical and chemical events must occur in order for your finger to move.

All muscle movement involves a complex process of sending and receiving chemical and electrical signals inside the body.

To start, the brain forms the thought that you want to wiggle your finger. An electrical impulse travels from the brain and down your spinal cord to motor neurons located near muscles. Motor neurons electrically stimulate nearby muscle fibers at a place called the neuromuscular junction. Acetylcholine gets released between the motor neuron and the muscle fiber and attaches to the muscle fiber. An electrical charge then causes muscle fibers to contract. Your finger muscles move and your finger wiggles.

Your brain also controls involuntary process like digestion. Deep in your brain stem, motor neurons cause smooth muscles to move food throughout the digestive system. Because it is involuntary, this takes place whether you think about it or not.

The brain also communicates with sensory neurons located in the autonomic nervous system (ANS). This involuntary system also makes muscles move. When sensory neurons detect changes that affect muscles, the brain swings into gear. It sends out electrical and neurotransmitter messages to motor neurons. They activate muscles to take action. Step back from the curb! Pull your hand away from the hot stove! Stop running!

Do Muscles Have Memories?

With a lot of help from the brain, muscles have a kind of memory that experts call brain-muscle, or neuromuscular memory. The process begins with chemical and electrical activities inside the brain. For example, a person has the thought, "I want to shoot this basketball into the hoop." Motor neurons activate neurotransmitter chemicals to carry that message to muscle cells throughout the body to perform the action. After a lot of practice—raising the ball towards the basket, for example—this neuromuscular process happens so fast, it seems automatic. The muscles have learned how to do this and can do it quickly, over and over again.

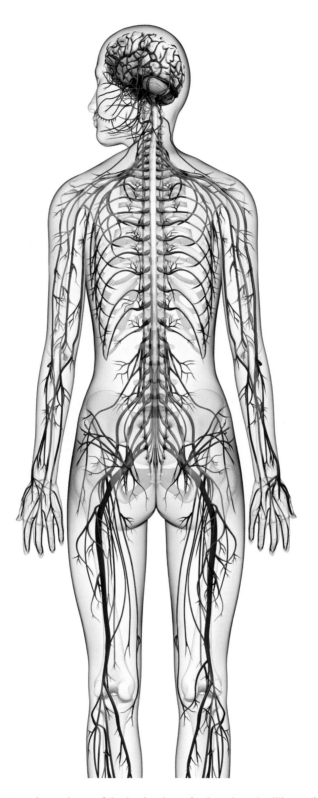

The nervous system is made up of the brain, the spinal cord, and millions of nerves that run throughout the body.

Your muscle systems are always hard at work, allowing you to balance your body, speak, smile, and even breathe.

Muscle memory requires food and rest. If you are tired, or have not eaten, the chemical processes involved in muscle memory slow down. Your energy level drops. You may feel weak or forget what you meant to say. To strengthen your muscle memory and keep your muscles in good working order, you must have proper nutrients and enough rest.

As you read along, your three muscles systems are working quietly. Head and neck muscles are holding your head up to read. If you just came in from a fast workout in gym, your cardiac muscles sent extra blood to your muscles. If you just drank a glass of water, smooth muscles will get the oxygenated water to cells throughout your body to keep muscles hydrated. All the while, you barely have to think about any this. The muscle activities happen so smoothly, you can just keep on reading.

RIGOR MORTIS

When death comes to a human or any other animal, the body stiffens into a condition called rigor mortis. These Latin words mean "rigidity of death." In a live body, certain chemicals move in and out of muscles to help them tighten and expand. Death stops this process. Without chemical movement, muscles cannot relax. They remain stiff.

Rigor mortis first stiffens small facial muscles. Then other small muscles in the neck, shoulders, and arms tighten. The larger muscles of the back, abdomen, and lower body stiffen later.

Rigor mortis is a temporary condition. After several days, other chemical processes involving decay cause the muscles to loosen again. Forensic scientists, who study the causes of death, can often determine approximately when someone died by studying the stage of rigor mortis in the body's muscles.

2

Muscles on the Go

Our bodies would go haywire if individual muscles and the three muscles systems acted on their own. Fortunately, in a healthy body, muscles and their three systems work together efficiently

THE SKELETAL MUSCLE SYSTEM

Without skeletal muscles, bones would hang as loosely as a Halloween skeleton. Of the three muscle systems, skeletal muscles are the volunteers. When we tell them what to do—wave, jump, or

◀ *Skeletal muscle is sometimes called striated muscle because of the bands, or striations, formed by muscle fibers.*

kick—skeletal muscles and their connecting tissues pull on our bones, and they move.

The majority of muscles in the body, around 650 of them, are part of the skeletal muscle system. Muscles in the skeletal muscle system have unique features. Their cells, are long and rod shaped. While other kinds of cells contain one control center called a nucleus, each skeletal muscle cell may have hundreds, even thousands, of nuclei. Skeletal muscle cells are arranged near the surface along the length of each muscle fiber. This gives skeletal muscle tissue the ability to bend, stretch, and shorten quickly. Almost anything you tell your muscles to do activates skeletal muscles. You can see many of them move as they carry out orders.

AXIAL MUSCLES

Without moving your arms or legs, turn your head. Now twist your upper body. Axial skeletal muscles in the head, neck, and trunk (upper body) make that kind of pivoting motion possible. Axial muscles make up about 60 percent of the skeletal muscle system. They protect, support, and cause movement in the skull, rib cage, and backbone.

Axial muscles are at work when you stick out your tongue, frown, smile, or lower your eyelids. They enable you to shake your head, move it sideways, forward, and back. Axial muscles in the neck allow you to swivel your neck as well as bend it backward and forward. If you bend forward or backward at the waist, torso axial muscles make that happen.

Head and Face Muscles

Facial muscles in the skeletal muscle system enable us to make faces and express feelings without using words. These muscles are anchored on the

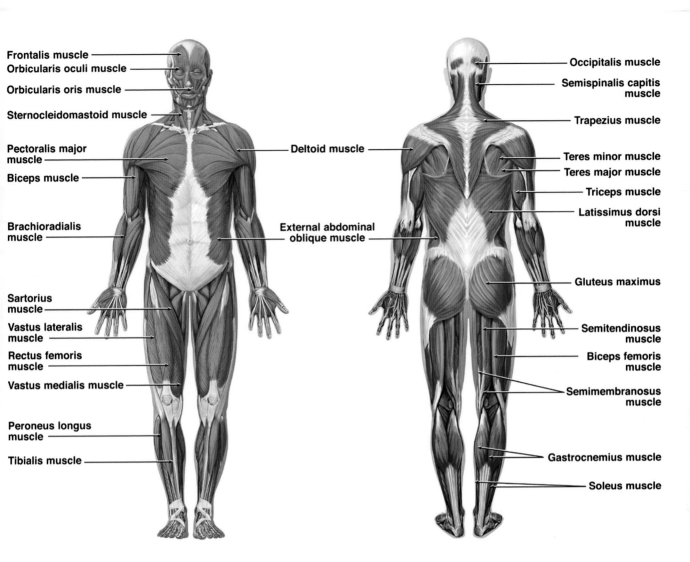

These illustrations label many of the body's skeletal muscles.

skull at one end of the muscle and to facial skin on the other. Layers of facial muscles stretch across the skull and other tissues that are part of the face. Facial nerves activate them. Arteries near the head supply facial muscles with blood.

Six extraocular muscles control eye movements, such as rolling your eyes to look in different directions. The muscles that move the eye are called orbicularis oculi. Some are skeletal eye muscles that we can direct. (Eye muscles responsible for focusing, involuntary blinking, and automatically lowering eyelids during sleep are made of involuntary smooth muscles.) Full eyelid action involves areas in the forehead, above the bridge of the nose, and the temples. Eye muscles move about 100,000 times a day.

The smallest muscles in the body are located inside the ears. Two of them move tiny bones in the middle ear that carry or block sound.

Frontalis muscles run across the forehead from the scalp to the eyebrows. These forehead muscles mainly lift or "scrunch" the eyebrows. They are involved in the expression of such emotions as surprise and worry. Constant use of frontalis muscles may cause the skin of the forehead to wrinkle as people age.

If you touch your temple while chewing food, you can feel your temporalis facial muscles at work. They pull up the upper jaws during chewing and let them down afterwards. Temporalis muscles run from the sides of the head, arch over the ears, and end near the upper jaw. When people express tense feelings by clenching their teeth, they tighten their temporalis muscle at the same time.

Small but powerful masseter muscles below the jawbones make it possible to chew food and to speak. Masseter muscles are often involved when someone is tense or angry. Happier feelings show up on the face as a smile thanks to zygomaticus muscles, which pulls the upper lip upwards. These "smiling" muscles run from the upper corners of the mouth to the cheekbone.

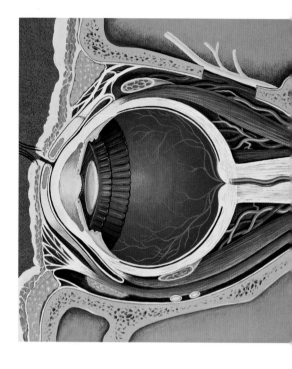

Some muscles—shown here as red bundles above and below the eye— control which direction the eyeball moves. Other types of muscles inside the eyes help with vision.

Think of all the jobs your mouth does. It can make faces that express all kinds of feelings. It can form words, sip, chew, or whistle a tune. Multiple muscles coordinate in and around the mouth and lips to perform these actions. Orbicularis oris muscles surrounding the lips are made up of crisscrossing fibers from other facial muscles as well as fibers unique to these mouth muscles. Orbicularis oris make up the round sphincter mouth muscles.

Sphincter muscles are types of round muscles that loosen and tighten. Some sphincters, such as around the mouth and outside part of the bladder, can be voluntarily controlled to keep in or release fluids and other substances. Other sphincter muscles—such as those found in the digestive tract—are involuntary and contract and relax to move food and other substances.

The tongue may look like one big muscle. However, it is made up of many small bundles of muscle fibers anchored at one end. These muscle bundles are responsible for

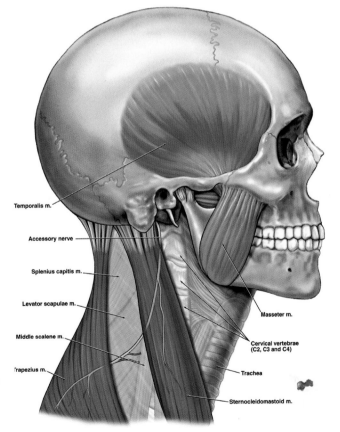

Temporalis m.

Accessory nerve

Splenius capitis m.

Levator scapulae m.

Middle scalene m.

Masseter m.

Cervical vertebrae (C2, C3 and C4)

Trapezius m.

Trachea

Sternocleidomastoid m.

The muscles of the face and neck help you turn your head, chew, and make facial expressions.

BOTULINUM AND BOTOX

The botulinum bacteria, which are tiny microorganisms, can cause botulism, a form of food poisoning so severe that it paralyzes a victim's chest muscles, making it hard to breathe. However, a variation of the botulism poison—in small doses—goes by its well-known commercial name, Botox. Doctors carefully use Botox injections to treat several medical conditions that involve muscle movement and painful muscle contractions called spasms. Botox can sometimes relieve back and neck pain by slightly paralyzing certain muscles near the spine that are tightened too much.

However, the most common use of Botox in the last decade has been for cosmetic reasons, not medical ones. Skin doctors, and other medical practitioners, administer Botox injections to people who want to smooth out facial wrinkles. Botox does the job by temporarily paralyzing the facial muscles. The cosmetic effect of this paralysis can last for several months. The most popular site for cosmetic Botox facial injections is the forehead. However, many people who have such injections lose some facial expression since they are unable to move their eyebrow muscles.

Botox works the way botulism does. Its poisons prevent the release of acetylcholine, one of the chemical substances that make muscles move. When muscles are paralyzed, they cannot tighten or cause the skin to wrinkle. However, using Botox can cause side effects such as flu-like symptoms, trouble swallowing, or headaches. Using too much Botox can also permanently damage the muscle or even cause death. A qualified medical professional should always be the one to administer Botox injections.

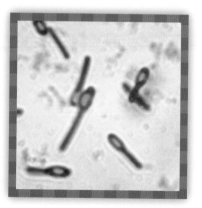

Botulinum bacteria

countless movements of the tongue. Some bundles, along the surface of the tongue, aid in speech. Others are located in the bottom or back of the tongue. These help to raise, lower, or push the tongue to form words, chew food, break it down for digestion, and push it towards smooth muscles in the throat. Other mouth muscles are located on the roof and floor of the mouth. Still others are located in the cheeks. These all play a role in speech and in digestion.

Neck Muscles

Neck muscles hold up your head and allow you to rotate it so you can see and hear things coming from different directions. Neck muscles also protect the passageways for vocal chords, the esophagus (a part of the digestive system), and windpipe (part of your respiratory system). These muscles move and protect the bones in the upper spine and chest. If you run your fingers from the bony bumps behind your ears all the way down to your collarbones, you will find two paired muscles. These are the cordlike sternocleidomastoid muscles (SCM). They not only make it possible for you to rotate and flex your head, they act as brakes so your head does not fall backwards. Pairs of scalene muscles also run along the sides of your neck. They aid in breathing. They do this by pulling on upper ribs, allowing lungs to expand as they take in air.

The diaphragm is the main muscle involved in breathing. Contraction of the diaphragm causes a person to breathe in. When this sheet-like muscle expands, the person can breathe out. The diaphragm muscle also separates the heart and lungs from the stomach, liver, and intestines.

Trunk Muscles

Body builders often call the upper chest muscles "pecs." This is the nickname for pectoralis major. This pair of large axial skeletal muscles fans across the front of the upper torso. In females, the pectoral muscles lie below the breasts. Pecs help to move shoulders move back and forth and keep the arms close to the body. Exercise can increase the size of pectoral muscles.

"Abs" is the nickname for rectus abdominus. These axial skeletal muscles run like a large

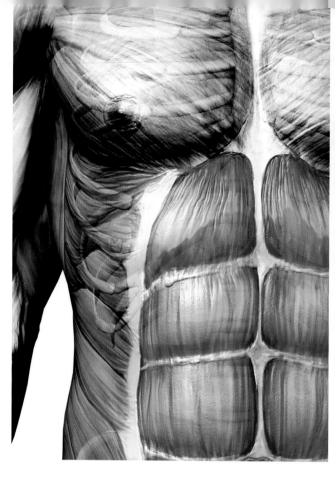

Diet and the proper exercises can give muscles like the abs more strength and better definition.

belt or strap across the abdomen. They begin at the ribs and go down to the pelvis near the hips. Abs support the stomach, organs, and bones in the torso. Abs also make it possible for the trunk to bend and twist. Exercising these muscles can cause abs to become stronger and have a very defined look, which many body builders try to achieve.

Muscles are hard at work in the back of the torso, too. Trapezius muscles stretch from the neck to the middle of the back. They allow the shoulders to move up and down, while keeping them attached to the body. Another set of back muscles, latissimus dorsi, support the lower back and help rotate the arms. All skeletal back muscles protect and support organs in the torso, such as the kidneys and spinal column bones. By pulling on these spinal bones, muscles enable the spine to rotate, twist, and bend.

DISTAL MUSCLES

While head and trunk muscles move within the trunk core, distal muscles can move away from the core. Distal muscles include the muscles in the shoulders, arms, hips, and legs.

If you touch the rounded tops of your shoulders, you can feel your deltoids. These fan-shaped muscles are involved in pressing, flexing or bending, and moving arms away from the body. They assist pectoral muscles in moving bones in the chest and arms. Different kinds of weight-lifting exercises can build up the deltoids.

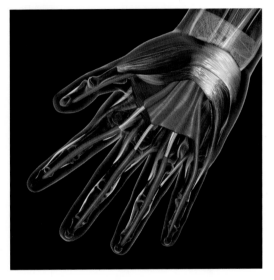

Biceps braccii are the two bundles of upper arm muscles that people tighten if asked to show the muscles of their upper arms. These biceps are involved in rotating the arm or bending the elbow. Straighten out your arm, and you can feel muscles tighten. These are

Muscles branch from the forearm to the wrist and into the hand. Different-sized muscles allow for various movements—from a strong grip to a gentle touch.

the triceps braccii. Triceps make up the highest percentage of muscle in the arm. Exercise can build up biceps and triceps.

The thin, long muscles of the forearm move hand bones in different ways. Some straighten out the fingers and wrist. Other forearm muscles bend bones in the hand.

Leg and hip muscles do the body's heavy lifting. They hold up the body against the gravity that would pull it to the ground.

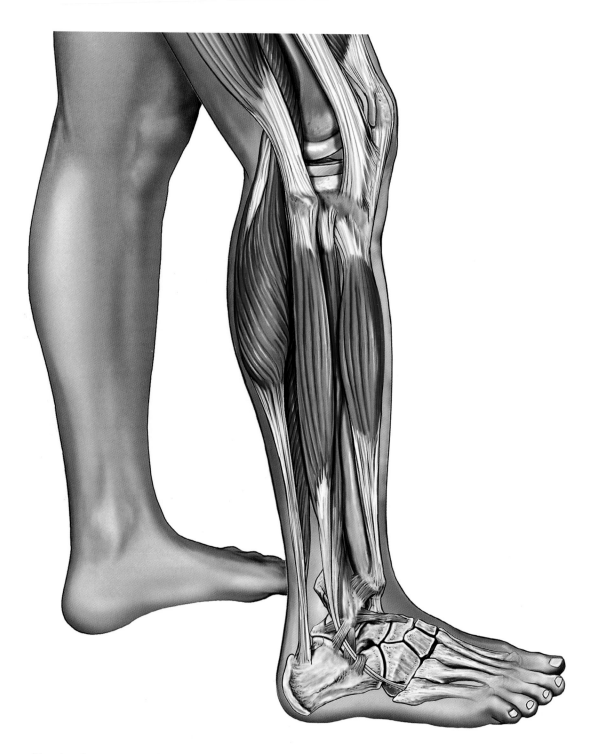

Muscles, ligaments, tendons, and bones work together to move and support body parts.

The muscles in your thighs are much larger than the muscles in your arms. The skeletal muscles of the lower body have to support themselves, the bones they move, as well as the entire upper body. This is why leg and hip muscles are larger and more powerful than arm muscles.

Leg muscles do more than support the body. They move hips, knees, and feet. The thigh muscles on the front of legs are the quadriceps. These four grouped muscles straighten the knees. Hamstrings on the back of legs are the muscles that cause the knee to bend. Adductor muscles are the ones you feel on your inner thighs when you sit cross-legged. Other muscles involving the thighs are the long, strap-like sartorius muscles. Each starts just above the thigh, runs down and across it, and ends in the calf. It allows you to rotate your leg.

Calf muscles, and Achilles tendons attached to them, make it possible for you to rotate your feet. At the front of your legs—your shins—are the tibialis anterior muscles. They bring up your foot when you run.

Are you sitting down? If so, then the strongest muscles in your body, the gluteus maximus muscles are supporting you. These buttock muscles are not just cushions for keeping you comfortable while sitting. They get your hips moving when you jump up and down or climb up stairs.

SMOOTH MUSCLES

Muscle movement in smooth muscle system is hidden and mainly involuntary. That is because smooth muscles are located within structures and organs deep inside the body. They are organized in layers that move against one another.

Arteries, veins, and capillaries that carry blood are lined with smooth muscles. The digestive system, which includes the stomach, esophagus, intestines, and anus are made of smooth muscles. So are the bladder, urethra, and ureter tubes that hold in or release urine. Smooth muscles also make up parts of the respiratory system involved in breathing. Some smooth muscles focus eyes for seeing as well as control automatic eyelid movements.

Blood Vessels

Smooth muscles line the walls of all the vessels that move blood through the body—tiny capillaries, larger veins, and even larger arteries. When smooth muscles in blood vessels tighten too much, high blood pressure is the result. (Blood pressure is the measurement of the force at which blood is moving through the vessels.) When blood pressure is high, too much blood tries to squeeze through vessels that are too small. This can be caused by tightened muscles, but it can also be caused by substance buildup on the vessels' walls.

When smooth muscles in blood vessels relax too much due to excessive bleeding, certain diseases, or drug overdoses, a serious condition called shock can occur. During shock, smooth muscle cells cannot generate enough energy to move blood to organs and tissues that need it. As a result, cells in those structures collapse.

Digestive and Urinary Muscles

When you take a bite of a sandwich and chew it, the voluntary axial skeletal muscles in your mouth and jaws go to work. But as soon as you finish chewing and swallow your sandwich bite, smooth muscles take over.

Swallowed food moves into the esophagus, which is a tube lined with smooth muscles. Smooth muscle contractions within the esophagus push chewed food into the stomach. This pushing is called peristalsis.

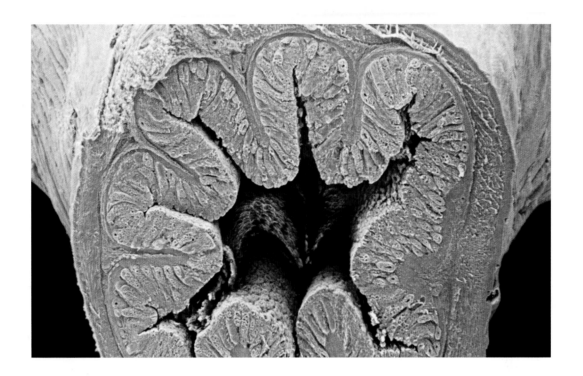

A cross-section of part of the large intestine shows the muscles that help to move food and nutrients through the digestive tract.

Inside the stomach, several layers of smooth muscles churn the chewed food. During this time, gastric acids and enzymes break down the food. Further peristalsis by the smooth muscles in the stomach moves processed liquids and solids into the small intestines. Tiny structures in the small intestines carry nutrients from the digested food into a vein lined with smooth muscles. The vein carries the nutrients to the liver where they undergo changes before entering the blood. Smooth sphincter muscles push liquid and solid waste from the body.

Reproductive Muscles

Smooth muscles line structures in the reproductive system. In males, smooth muscle contractions in three structures—the epididymis, vas deferens, and urethra—push sperm cells out of the body through the penis.

Smooth muscles line structures of the female reproductive system as well. Smooth muscles move along fertilized and unfertilized eggs from

Fibers in smooth muscle tissue slide back and forth against each other, creating involuntary movements that help carry necessary life processes.

ovaries into the uterus. If a sperm cell fertilizes an egg cell and it attaches to the uterus, a fetus will develop. When the fetus is fully grown and ready to be born, smooth sphincter muscles in the uterus will eventually contract to push out the fetus through the vaginal canal, which is also lined with smooth muscles. If a sperm cell does not fertilize an egg cell, the smooth muscles of the uterus push out unused uterine tissues as part of a female's menstrual cycle.

Smooth Eye Muscles

Focusing the eye is the job of the smooth cillary muscles. They shape the part of the eye called the lens that captures light. When the cillary muscles contract to make the lens thicker, they bend light rays to focus on close objects. To bring faraway objects into focus, these same smooth muscles stretch out the lens.

CARDIAC MUSCLE

The steadiest workhorses of the body's three muscle systems are the cardiac muscles, which are also called the myocardium. They line the walls of the heart. Twisted bundles of cardiac muscles are so interconnected that they almost behave as a single muscle. Like smooth muscles, healthy cardiac muscles work automatically within the autonomic nervous system.

When healthy, heart muscles work without resting. They steadily squeeze blood from the heart into the blood vessels at an average rate of

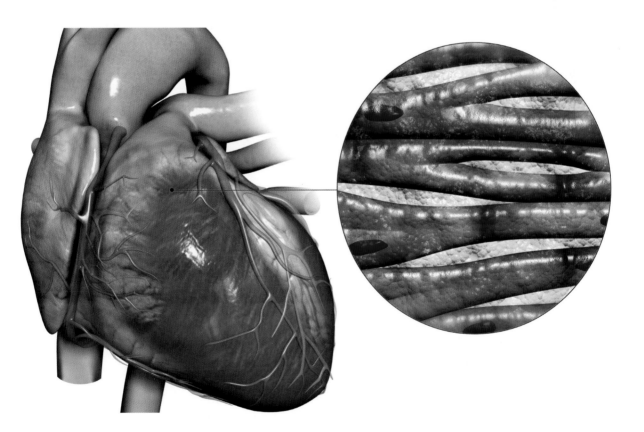

Smooth muscle fibers (right) join together to form the myocardium, or heart muscle.

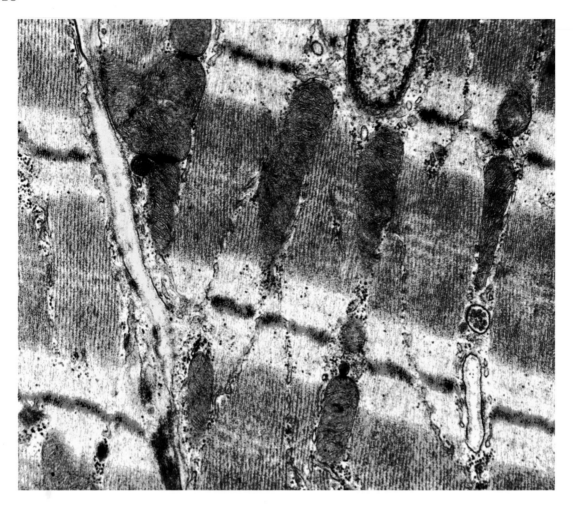

Cardiac muscle appears to have bands (stained different colors in this sample) that form a pattern through the muscle. These bands are made up of sarcomeres, or repeating units of muscle fibrils. Skeletal muscle also has bands, or striations, from sarcomeres.

seventy-two beats a minute in a healthy person. Cardiac muscles contract to pump out blood and relax to let blood into the heart.

Compared to muscles in the other two systems, cardiac muscles are self starters. They do not need nerves from the central nervous system (CNS) to stimulate them. A heart has its own self-contained electrical system. Electrical and chemical activity causes the heart to contract and expand.

Pacemaker cells generate electrical activity in the atrium of the heart. The electrical impulse travels through all the cardiac muscles almost simultaneously. This electrical activity causes the release of calcium ions into cardiac muscle cells. Calcium release causes myosin heads to pull on actin where these proteins overlap. The contraction that follows sends blood from the heart into the blood vessels. When calcium ions are depleted, the myosin and actin proteins disconnect. As a result, the cardiac muscles relax, and blood flows into the heart from the rest of the body. Without the actions of these cardiac muscles, your heart would stop, and your body would die.

SKELETAL MUSCLE	SMOOTH MUSCLE	CARDIAC MUSCLE
Voluntary movement	Involuntary movement	Involuntary movement
Cause movement of bones	Cause movement of vessels and organs	Cause heartbeat to pump blood
Arranged in bundles	Arranged mainly in layers with some bundles	Arranged in twisted bundles
Striped	No stripes	Striped
Contract and expand quickly	Contract and expand slowly	Contract and expand steadily
Cell fibers have multiple nuclei	Cell fibers have one nucleus	Single nucleus
Stimulated by central nervous system (CNS)	Mainly stimulated by the autonomic nervous system (ANS)	Stimulated by the autonomic nervous system (ANS)

3

Muscle Diseases

Most healthy people do not have to think too much about their muscles. Muscles get so much blood, they usually do what they are supposed to do. They keep the body upright, toned, at the right temperature, and on the move. Unfortunately, things can go wrong in all three muscular systems.

MUSCULAR DYSTROPHY

The potential for developing a muscle disorder called muscular dystrophy (MD) is usually present at birth. The nine diffrent types of

This muscle tissue sample from a person affected by muscular dystrophy shows how the disease is replacing healthy muscle tissue (red and dark pink) with harmful fat deposits (light pink and w hite).

muscular dystrophy are mainly due to certain inherited genes. Genes are units of information in cells that a parent passes on to a child. Sometimes gene abnormalities, called mutations, occur. The genes of someone with muscular dystrophy have a characteristic that causes skeletal muscles to deteriorate. This happens because a protective muscle protein, called dystrophin, is completely absent in muscle cells. Or the affected person's muscle cells may do not have enough dystrophin to protect muscle fibers and keep them strong and healthy.

The two major forms of muscular dystrophy are Duchenne's Muscular Dystrophy (DMD) and Becker's Muscular Dystrophy (BMD). Young males usually inherit this genetic defect from their mothers, who carry the gene, but do not have MD themselves. MD is not preventable.

The most common and difficult form of MD is Duchenne's. Each year about 1 in 3000 male infants is born with Duchenne's in the United States. Approximately 200,000 individuals live with DMD. The symptoms usually appear before an affected boy is six years old. The child may have trouble learning to walk, climb stairs, or

Muscular dystrophy causes many different disabilities, but that does not stop many from participating in activities. This woman's arms and legs are affected by MD, but she has found other ways to paint.

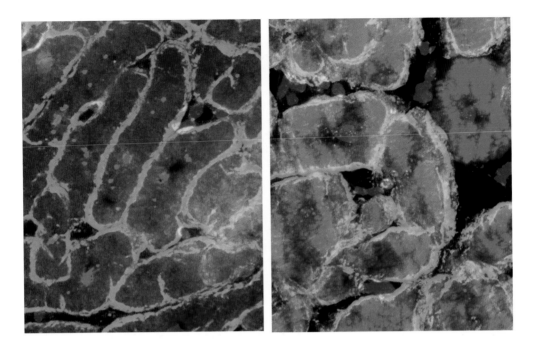

Dystrophin deficiencies can also be found in cardiac muscle. Healthy cardiac muscle (left) has plenty of dystrophin (green) surrounding the muscle (red). The image on the right is from a heart affected by muscular dystrophy. More black areas between muscle cells indicates less dystrophin.

run because pelvic and leg muscles are starting to deteriorate. The disorder eventually affects cardiac muscles as well as skeletal muscles that push air in and out of them. Without enough oxygen, the lungs of patients with Duchenne's often cannot fight off repeated respiratory infections.

Becker's Muscular Dystrophy causes many similar symptoms of muscle wasting as the Duchenne's form. BMD affects males, though at later ages than those with DMD. Males with BMD also experience heart problems because the disorder weakens cardiac muscles. However, BMD causes less severe symptoms than DMD.

There is no cure for either DMD or BMD, but there are different medical treatments that can help. Many new forms of physical therapy, as well as aids, such as special braces, wheelchairs, and breathing devices, help those with DMD and BMD.

NEUROMUSCULAR DISORDERS

Diseases and injuries that affect the brain, spine, and neurons can prevent muscles from working properly. That is because the brain directs most muscle activity through nerves in the central and autonomic nervous systems.

Two muscle disorders that injure motor neurons develop in adults. The muscles of individuals with multiple sclerosis (MS) start off fine. However, MS damages the sheath, or covering, of motor neurons. As a result, the neurons do not transmit messages well. So messages from the brain do not reach muscles, which may weaken and deteriorate.

Special physical therapy helps many people with neuromuscular diseases. This woman and her physical therapist are doing special muscle exercises in a pool.

Faulty motor neurons also cause the muscle destroying disorder, amyotrophic lateral sclerosis (ALS). Someone in the earliest stages of ALS may have trouble with controlled movements in the arms and legs—walking, picking up objects, or writing. As ALS worsens, it affects involuntary muscles such as those involved in breathing. The majority of people with ALS die from the disease when they cannot take in enough oxygen to survive, even with a breathing machine. The causes of MS and ALS are not fully known.

ALS is often called Lou Gehrig's Disease after the famous baseball player who was affected by the disease.

Parkinson's disease is a central nervous system disorder that usually affects bones, joints, muscles, and all their movements. The loss of dopamine, an important chemical in the central nervous system, disrupts pathways to and from the brain and other parts of the body, including muscles. Muscles may become rigid. Speech may be affected when tongue muscles weaken. Affected individuals are usually older adults over the age of sixty. Medication and some forms of therapy can help people with Parkinson's, though there is no cure for the disease.

Two disorders affect muscles in the head. A condition called myasthenia gravis develops when infection fighters called antibodies mistakenly attack the part of healthy muscle fibers that take in the acetylcholine that makes the muscles contract. When muscles cannot tighten, they get weak. In myasthenia gravis, the weakness primarily shows up in the head muscles. Individuals with myasthenia gravis may not be able to speak, chew, or swallow normally, or move their eyes at will. There is general muscle weakness that may also affect breathing. Therapy, medication, and other aids can help many people with myasthenia gravis.

An injury to a nerve inside the head can temporarily cause Bell's Palsy facial paralysis. This nerve damage prevents the release of certain chemicals muscle fibers need to contract. A person, usually someone older, may wake up, unable to move half of his or her face. Though sudden and frightening, the facial paralysis of Bell's Palsy usually reaches a peak in several days. In most cases, all symptoms usually go away on their own within two weeks.

A stroke in the brain can cause a victim to lose muscle control. It occurs when a blood vessel in the brain ruptures or gets blocked. Risk factors for stroke include smoking, obesity, high blood pressure, diabetes, and a family history of strokes. Strokes often produce many unpredictable symptoms—double vision, speech problems, and paralysis on one side of the body. Eye muscles may not be able to focus. The person's mouth muscles may not be able to form words, chew, or swallow. Arm, hand, leg, or foot muscles may not be able to move at all. Quick medical treatment and new physical therapies have improved the outcomes for many stroke victims.

PERIPHERAL NEUROPATHIES

Some muscle disorders are due to problems with the sensory neurons, which send messages from the skin, joints, and muscles, to the brain. (This part of the nervous system is called the peripheral nervous system.)

The nervous and muscle systems are closely connected. Many muscle fibers (pink) have nerve cells (dark threads) attached or next to them. The nerve cells transmit commands to the muscles. Neuropathies can interfere with neuromuscular communications, causing problems with muscle control.

Because the nerves are damaged or destroyed, someone with a peripheral neuropathy may have muscle pain, numbness, or an inability to control certain muscles. The causes may be one of many medical conditions, such as diabetes or a tick-borne illness, such as Lyme disease. A neuropathy may develop after excessive pressure or an injury to a joint or muscle. Some nerves can repair themselves and improve, but sometimes nerves are damaged beyond repair. Certain medical therapies and treatments can help with some forms of peripheral neuropathy.

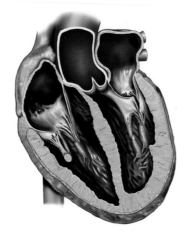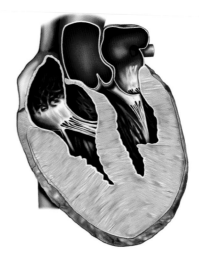

Normal heart
(cut section)

Heart muscle becomes
too thick (hypertrophy)

Certain disorders can cause heart muscle to be too thick (right). If the cardiac muscles are too thick, the heart is not able to efficiently pump blood, causing many other problems in the body.

CARDIAC MUSCLE DISEASE

The causes are not completely known. They may include infection of the heart muscle, a previous heart attack, alcoholism, smoking, long-term high blood pressure, and possible inherited heart abnormalities. Unlike other heart disorders that usually affect older people, cardiomyopathy can sometimes strike young people. A healthy lifestyle may prevent some, but not all, cases of cardiomyopathy.

MUSCLE INFLAMMATION DISEASE

Symptoms of several skeletal muscle disorders, called myopathies, include weakness and sometimes pain and a rash. Three myopathies are due to inflammation, or swelling of blood vessels inside muscle tissues. Most experts believe these myopathies develop because antibodies that are supposed to attack infectious intruders attack the body instead.

Dermatomyositis and polymyositis affect adults. Juvenile myositis affects nearly five thousand children a year in the United States between the ages of five to fifteen. The symptoms begin with a skin rash as well as muscle weakness. A child's or teen's muscles are so weak, he or she cannot get out of a chair or climb a flight of stairs. He or she may feel overwhelmingly tired and may have trouble swallowing. A reddish, almost purple rash, may appear around the eyes, on the knees, and around the elbows.

Many children with muscle diseases are still able to go to school and take part in different activities. Some help or physical aid, such as a wheelchair, may be needed to help them move around.

None of the myopathies is preventable or curable yet, but they are manageable. Medication can slow the progress of the autoimmune attack that is causing the muscle inflammation.

MUSCLE TUMORS

Like other parts of the body, muscles can develop clusters of abnormal cells called tumors. As tumors grow, they may invade and spread to other

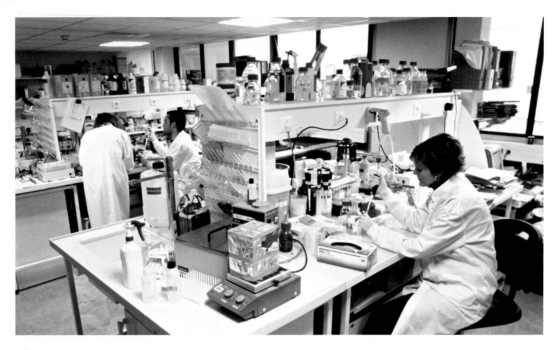

Scientists and researchers continue to search for ways to better diagnose and cure muscle diseases.

tissues. Less harmful benign tumors can grow within tissues but do not spread into others.

Benign smooth muscles tumors can start to grow in intestines, blood vessels, and other parts of the body that are lined with smooth muscles. One type of smooth muscle tumor, called fibroid uterine tumors, are somewhat common in women. Most benign tumors are removed surgically and usually do not cause other problems.

Malignant cancerous muscle tumors are far more harmful. They may arise in skeletal muscles, sometimes deep inside arm and leg muscles. Depending upon the type of cancer, surgery or other medical treatments may be performed to treat the cancer.

Rhabdomyosarcomas are a rare kind of skeletal muscle tumor that mainly affects about 350 infants and children a year in the United States. Some children inherit a tendency to develop such cancers. Most often, though, the causes are unknown. Chemotherapy (cancer-killing) medication and surgery are often used to remove these types of tumors.

POISONING

Like any other part of the body, muscles can be poisoned. Botulism and tetanus poisoning are the most well known. About a hundred or so people get botulism poisoning in the United States each year. Around fifty people get tetanus poisoning. The poisons come from bacteria that enters the body through spoiled food or dirt. Botulism and tetanus bacteria release poisons that prevent the release of chemicals muscles need to move. Both types of bacteria cause life-threatening paralysis in all three muscle systems. The poisoned person cannot move at all, even to breathe. He or she may suffocate and die.

Preventing both types of poisoning is easier than curing them. People should avoid eating unwashed fruits and vegetables and spoiled food. Food should be cooked thoroughly and eaten hot then promptly refrigerated. Botulism can often be found in canned food that has spoiled. Cleaning and protecting wounds and cuts can help prevent the tetanus bacteria from entering the body. Tetanus vaccines, which are a kind of injection, are routinely given to people and have greatly cut down the number of deaths due to tetanus poisoning in the United States.

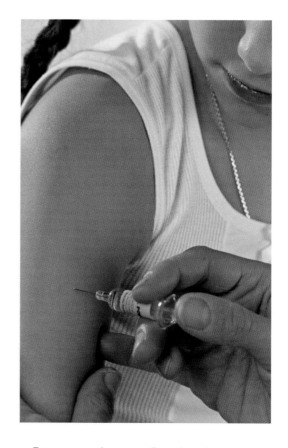

Tetanus vaccines are often given to prevent serious infections from the tetanus bacteria.

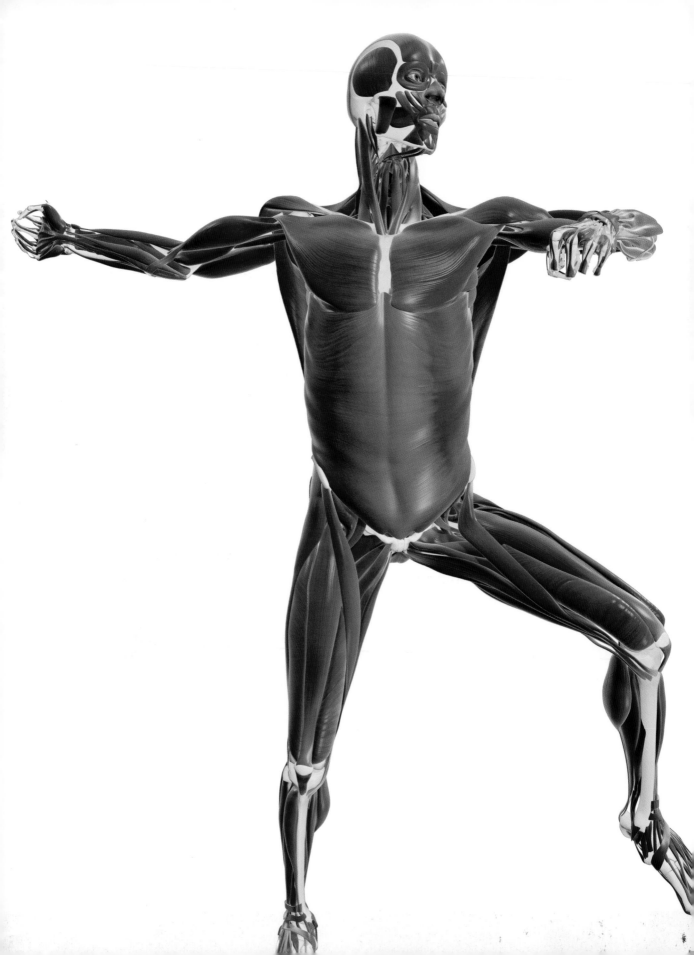

4

Muscle Injuries

The most common causes of muscle problems are injuries. A person injures a muscle or a group of muscles by doing a physical activity too long, too often, too quickly, or without preparing the muscles beforehand. The good news is that many muscle injuries can be prevented. And if they develop, minor injuries can be treated at home. With ice, an over-the-counter pain reliever, and rest, most injured muscles usually heal within a few days.

Muscles allow us to run, jump, dance, and play sports. But overusing them can cause painful injuries.

MUSCLE SORENESS

You probably know how sore muscles feel. A great game you are playing runs into overtime, you keep playing baseball, softball, or basketball long after the sun goes down, or you did too many repetitions with weights at the gym. The exercise felt great while you were doing it, so why not do more? But hours later, or the next day, you can barely walk or lift your arm to brush your teeth. Your arm or calf muscles are screaming in pain. Two days later, you may still be limping around. What happened?

Exercise and physical activities are good for building muscles, but working your muscles too hard can cause painful injuries or serious damage.

This condition is called delayed onset muscle soreness (DOMS). It happens when someone over-exercises certain muscles. Leg and arm muscles are more likely to develop DOMS than other muscle groups. DOMS usually hits when someone is starting a new sport too quickly. The early days of spring or fall training are prime times for developing DOMS when people do not slowly get into shape beforehand or when someone doing a previous activity starts doing a lot more of it. Many sports medicine experts believe that tiny muscle tears, plus inflammation, cause the soreness.

Following these steps can often prevent DOMS. Warm up before any physical activity to get good blood flow to your muscles. Five or ten minutes of jumping jacks, slow jogging, or fast walking are good aerobic warm-ups that send oxygenated blood to muscles. Do major physical activities a few times a week instead of during weekend bursts. This gives your muscles a chance to get conditioned. Increase activity levels in new and old sports slowly, 10 percent at a time. That means if you have been practicing an hour with no pain, just add another six minutes at a time. If you would like to add another mile to running, just run a tenth of a mile more a day until you reach your goal without soreness. Or add a one-pound weight if you usually do weightlifting exercises with ten-pound weights.

If you do happen to get DOMS after a too-fast, too-long workout, here are some tips for dealing with muscle soreness. Stop doing the activity. DOMS usually goes away on its own after a few days. If you want to stay in shape despite the soreness, do some unrelated very slow activity like walking to keep up blood flow to your muscles. Massage your aching muscles gently.

Rest, Ice, Compression, Elevating (RICE)

Sports medicine experts recommend four important steps to take when muscles get injured. **R**est immediately after an injury to prevent further damage. During rest and sleep, the body releases healing chemicals to help muscles recover. Apply **I**ce to injured muscles regularly during the course of twenty-four hours to reduce swelling. Wrap ice packs, a bag of ice cubes—or frozen veggies—in a cloth before putting it on the skin. **C**ompress, or wrap an Ace bandage or cloth around the throbbing muscle for a few days after an injury. **E**levate, or put your injured body part higher than your heart to get good blood flow going to the muscle.

An ice pack can help to ease some of the pain from muscle soreness.

RICE techniques, along with over-the-counter pain relievers can help ease the pain. Always be sure to take the recommended doses of pain relievers with adult supervision. If healing does not seem to be taking place after several days, you should seek medical treatment.

MUSCLE STRAINS

Pulled muscles, or strains, can cause sudden pain, muscle weakness, spasms, and swelling. These strains happen when muscle fibers become damaged, tear, or are too stretched out. The tears may be due to pressure on the muscle, sudden twisting, overuse, or lifting heavy weights too fast or too awkwardly. Muscle strains can be mild or completely disabling. They can happen anywhere in the body. However, three particular muscle strains can sideline injured people for weeks.

Groin muscle strains can occur during any activity that puts a lot of strain on inner thigh muscles. A severe groin pull can make it impossible for the injured person to walk until the muscle is repaired, or it heals. Special groin exercises can help strengthen these muscles so that they are less likely to get injured.

Back muscle strains anytime someone stretches back muscles too far. When that happens, the injured person may not be able to move or even get out of bed for a few days. Adults are much more likely to suffer from back muscle strains than children or adolescents. Risk factors include being out of shape, being overweight, and not lifting heavy

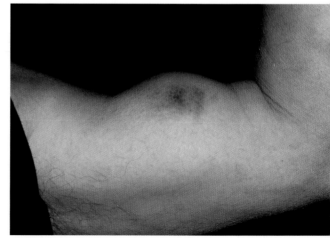

This person has torn a muscle in his bicep. The bruise and bump is a result of blood damaged and swollen blood vessels.

objects properly. So getting in shape, maintaining a healthy body weight, and lifting objects by bending at the knees—or getting a helper—can all help prevent back pain due to muscle strains. Doctors used to advise bed rest for severe back pain. However, after using RICE techniques—rest, ice, compression, and elevation—many experts now recommend gentle movement and specific exercises after a few days to strengthen back muscles.

Neck muscle strains occur when neck muscles snap or stretch too far. The cause may be an accident that causes whiplash. Or it may be as simple as sleeping with your head in a twisted position. Anyone who has been in an accident, or anyone with severe neck pain, should seek medical treatment right away.

Seeking medical treatment for any muscle injury is important if someone cannot move the body part where a muscle was injured. Some muscle tears are so serious that they require surgery to repair the muscle. Muscle numbness, reinjury to a muscle, or a hot, tender muscle should be seen by a doctor.

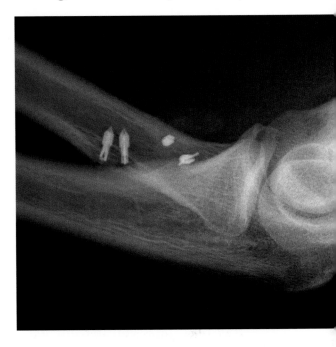

Sometimes serious muscle tears require surgery. This X ray shows small devices that were surgically inserted into a person's arm in order to pull torn muscles back together.

MUSCLE CRAMPS

It often happens out of the blue. You may be feeling fine while, running, swimming, biking, or playing ball. Seemingly out of nowhere, a knife

Gentle massage helps to ease the pain of most muscle cramps.

like pain jabs you in your leg, abdomen, shoulder, or arm. You may even be awoken in the middle of the night by muscle pains in your legs. Just about everyone occasionally gets abdominal cramps that come with an upset stomach.

A cramp, or series of them, takes place when a smooth muscle or an entire muscle group in your body suddenly seizes up involuntarily. The most common locations for cramps are the thigh muscles, either in the hamstrings in the back of the thigh, or the quadriceps at the front. However, no muscle group is spared from cramping. The back of the thigh, abdomen, back, neck, shoulders, hands, and feet can all cramp up. Fortunately, most muscle cramps do not last for long.

The exact cause of most cramps is not known. Abdominal cramps are associated with intestinal problems brought on by infection or food poisoning. The digestive muscles become involved as the body tries to rid itself of the virus or bacteria causing the stomach problems.

Muscle cramps often seem to happen during exercise or shortly afterwards. Many sport experts, therefore, believe lack of conditioning, stiffness, or overtraining can cause cramps. Cramps are more common when people work out in hot weather. The loss of certain chemicals in the body due to sweating is associated with muscle cramps. To function well, muscles need fluids, particularly electrolytes. These chemicals contain salts, potassium, magnesium, and calcium. Sweating and urination carry these important

Gently bending and stretching sore or cramping muscles can help during exercise. If the pain is too much, you should stop the activity and give your muscles time to rest and heal.

chemicals out of the body during and after heavy exercise. The body may also become dehydrated due to insufficient intake of water. Dehydration is associated with muscle cramps.

Using common sense can prevent most cramps. Get in shape before starting any major sport. Do short warm-ups to send blood to muscles before the activity. Stay hydrated by drinking plenty of water ahead of your thirst. Frequent cramping or excessively painful cramps should be checked out by a doctor.

5

Building Healthy Muscles

Muscles in the skeletal, smooth, and cardiac systems are the engines that keep your body moving. Like any engines, muscles need fuel and care to keep going. Think about what would happen to a car if no one changed the oil, water, and engine fluids, or if you forgot to put gas in the tank, or kept the engine running too long. Even a new car would soon stop working.

One great thing about taking good care of muscles is that you can see and feel positive results pretty quickly. Sports coaches know this

To stay healthy, muscles need regular exercise.

Anabolic steroids may increase muscle size in the long run, but they can also do great damage to the body.

and have their athletes get in shape during a week or two of preseason training. That training includes eating right, working out, and getting plenty of sleep.

BAD CHEMICALS

Smoking, drinking alcohol, and abusing drugs work against your body. These substances harm every cell in the body, including those in all three muscle systems. Nicotine in cigarettes damages smooth muscles in blood vessels and cardiac muscles in the heart. Alcohol is a depressant that slows down communication between the brain and all three muscle systems. This is why people stumble and mumble after they have been drinking. Alcohol even slows down digestive muscles in the smooth muscle system. Someone who has drunk too much may vomit because the slowed-down digestive muscles cannot process food. Illegal drug use or the misuse of prescription drugs can dangerously slow down or speed up communications between the brain and muscles.

Some athletes take anabolic steroids to build muscle mass and strength. These are manufactured copies of natural, muscle-building steroid hormones healthy people already have in their bodies. Side effects can include mood swings and aggression. Males taking steroids can develop abnormal growths of breast tissue and a shrinking of male sex organs. Women on artificial steroids may develop male characteristics, such as excess facial hair and a deeper voice.

A healthy body already makes the right amount of natural steroid hormones in the body to build strength, muscle mass, and reproductive organs. Many of these growth hormones get released during sleep. So anyone who wants to keep natural steroids at healthy levels should get plenty of regular sleep in addition to eating right and exercising.

FEEDING MUSCLES

Eating a wide variety of healthy foods that are low in fat, sugars, and salt are the best way to feed muscles. Healthy foods eaten at regular meal and snack times give muscles all the energy they need. Muscle-building foods include vegetables, beans, fruit, nuts, whole grain cereals, bread, pasta, as

The right amounts of fruits and vegetables can help your muscles grow.

well as soy or dairy products, fish, eggs, and lean meats and poultry. Many of these foods contain proteins, which muscle fibers are made of. Enriched dairy products and cereals contain Vitamin D, which has been shown in several studies to help strengthen muscles and ease muscle pain. Cereals, bread, and pasta, contain carbohydrates, which are used as stored energy in the muscles and liver. This is the fuel muscles burn for energy all the time, but especially during strenuous physical activity. Some athletes have learned to eat carbohydrates shortly after intense workouts to replace the energy they used up.

Certain vegetables and fruits contain muscle-promoting chemicals. Bananas, oranges, melons, broccoli, avocados, spinach, and eggplant are rich in potassium. Magnesium-rich foods include beans, especially soybeans, nuts, sweet potatoes, peanuts, oatmeal, and pumpkin seeds. Make sure to eat or drink low-fat foods with plenty of calcium, such as soy or cow's milk, yogurt, cheese. Salmon and sardines are high in calcium, too.

EXERCISING

Every part of the body gets stronger with regular exercise. Muscles, though, show fast, visible results within a couple weeks. Exercise builds muscles in two ways. First, exercise slightly injures the muscle bundles called sarcomeres. As a response, muscles make more fibers. So the muscles get bigger and stronger. Second, muscles burn up extra calories stored in fat cells. (Calories are units of fuel from the food we eat.) Muscles burn up those extra calories faster than fat cells do. As fat cells shrink down, muscles become more noticeable.

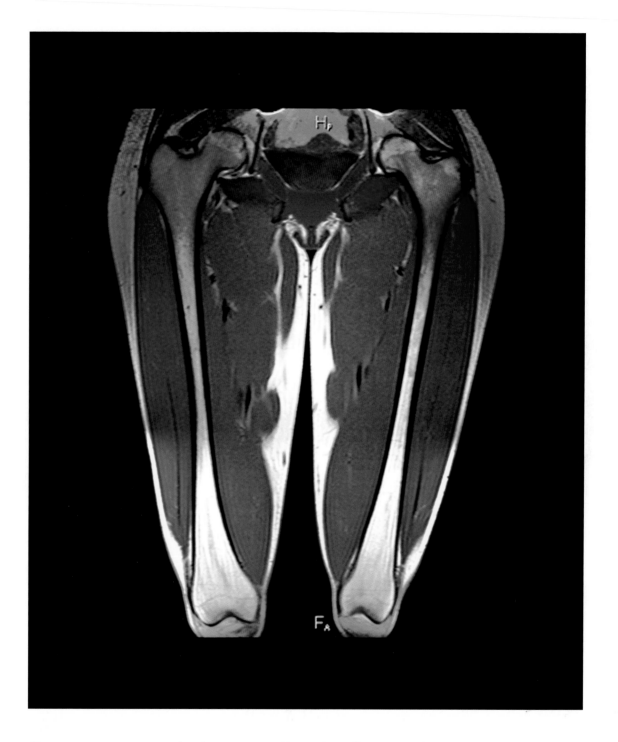

The more you use your muscles, the stronger and larger they will become. This colored scan of an athlete's upper legs shows how constant use has made the muscles bigger (purple).

Whenever you use heavy weights or other equipment to help you build muscle, you should follow the advice of trainers, coaches, and other experts. Exercising the wrong way can seriously damage your muscles.

Healthy exercise gives the muscles in the arms, legs, and the trunk a smooth, shaped look. This does not mean people should be trying for a bodybuilder appearance with bulging muscles. Overdoing exercise, like overdoing anything, is not a great idea. However, anyone who regularly exercises is doing a big favor to the heart and muscles. These kinds of aerobic exercises get the heart rate up so that it pumps more oxygen-rich blood to muscles.

Part of taking care of your muscles is resting them when they are tired or overworked and seeking medical help for injuries.

SLEEP AND MUSCLES

Healthy muscles are always working. However, they do need rest. Regular sleep every night gives them the break they need to repair worn-out cells. And during sleep, the body releases growth hormones, including natural steroids that build healthy muscles. Growth hormones affect the amount of muscle mass a person will have in relation to fat tissues. One study has shown that when young men did not get enough sleep, muscle mass decreased. They started to develop more belly fat in place of muscle.

TWITCHY MUSCLES

Athletes hope for it and train for it. It's that sudden burst of energy at a critical moment when they can sprint ahead in a competition. At the muscular level, such energy bursts come from fast-twitch muscle fibers. They make and release small amounts of energy quickly, without using oxygen. Fast-twitch muscles fire their energy during rapid movements, such as sprints, fast breaks, and the quick moves we make in daily life. Blinking is one of those fast moves, so eye muscles are made up of fast-twitch fibers.

Slow-twitch muscle fibers, on the other hand, are our everyday workhorses. They make energy slowly and steadily from oxygen. Because oxygen fuels the energy they make, slow-twitch muscles contain many more blood vessels than fast-twitch fibers. Slow-twitch muscles are active during long-distance walking, running, swimming, and other physical activities that require a constant, steady supply of energy. They do not tire as quickly as fast-twitch muscle fibers do.

Many experts believe that people inherit the number of slow-twitch and fast-twitch muscles they have. If that is true, then that means certain individuals are better suited to certain sports that involve more fast-twitch muscle fibers, such as sprinting. However, some scientific studies that show an individual who trains intensively in sports requiring fast motion can develop more fast-twitch muscles.

It is important to get enough restful sleep in a position in which you can relax your body and muscles. Falling asleep in an uncomfortable position can lead to muscle cramps or strains.

Many people who do not get enough sleep mistakenly think: "I can catch up on the weekend." In the deepest, latest stages of sleep, muscles barely move at all. These are the periods of cell repair and growth hormone release. When someone misses hours of sleep, they cannot make up that stage by sleeping later another night. So how much sleep is the right amount? Sleep specialists recommend that you sleep so that you

Staying fit and keeping your muscles in shape greatly helps with your overall health.

feel rested the next day and have the energy to do what you do on most days. A doctor or other health professional can advise you on how much sleep you should be getting each night. With good food, regular exercise, and enough sleep, your muscles will not let you down.

Glossary

acetylcholine—A chemical messenger, or neurotransmitter, that carries messages from the brain to the muscles.

actin—The protein in cells and muscle fibers, which works with the protein myosin to cause muscle contraction.

Adenosine Triphosphate (ATP)—A chemical compound in organisms that gives cells the energy to complete certain chemical changes.

autonomic nervous system (ANS)—The involuntary part of the nervous system that automatically controls functions of the body.

calcium ions—The molecules of a substance in all organisms that aids in muscle contraction.

capillaries—The smallest blood vessels that carry blood.

cardiomyopathy—A disorder in cardiac muscles, which may cause them to fail.

contract—To tighten or shorten.

fascicle—A bundle of muscle filaments.

filament—A threadlike structure inside muscle fibers.

glucose—A sugar the body produces from food, which muscles convert into energy.

muscle—The specialized tissue that produces movement, supports the skeleton, and moves fluids through the body by contracting and expanding.

muscle fiber—Muscles cells made of threadlike protein substances.

muscle spindle —A sensitive part of a muscle fiber that communicates information about muscles with the central nervous system.

myofibrils—Cylinder-shaped structures inside muscle cells that contain myofilaments.

myofilaments—Threadlike protein structures inside myofibrils.

myosin—A kind of protein inside muscles that cause them to contract.

neuromuscular—Pertaining to the relationship between nerves in the brain and muscles.

neuropathy—A disorder of nerves near the muscles.

neurotransmitter—A chemical messenger that carries signals from the brain's central nervous system to the rest of the body.

sarcomere—A bundled unit of thick and thin myofilaments involved in muscle contraction.

sensory neurons—Nerve cells near muscles that carry electrical impulses from the autonomic nervous system (ANS).

skeletal muscle system—The voluntary muscle group that moves bones.

smooth muscle system—The involuntary muscle group that moves organs and substances within the body.

tendon—The cordlike tissue that attaches muscles to bones and is made of collagen protein.

Bibliography

Dimon, Jr., Theodore and John Qualter. *Anatomy of a Moving Body: A Basic Course in Bones, Muscles, and Joints*. Berkeley, CA: North Atlantic Books, 2008.

....

Elderbrock, Mark and Cathy Fieseler. "Muscle Cramping in Endurance Races," *Running & FitNews*, June-August 2007.

....

Guynup, Sharon. "Masses of Muscles: Here's How They Work--And Why You Need to Keep Them in Tip-Top Shape." *Current Health 2*. April-May, 2007.

....

Jarmey, Chris. *The Concise Book of Muscles, Revised Edition*. Berkeley, CA: North Atlantic Books, 2008.

....

Medline: Bones, Joints, and Muscles. http://www.nlm.nih.gov/medlineplus/bonesjointsandmuscles.html

....

Myositis Center. http://www.hopkinsmedicine.org/myositis/myositis/.

....

Nelson, Arnold G. and Jouko Kokkonen ; illustrated by Jason M. McAlexander. *Stretching Anatomy*. Champaign, IL : Human Kinetics, 2007.

....

Sports Medicine. http://sportsmedicine.about.com/cs/injuries/a/doms.htm

....

Tiildus, Peter M., Editor. *Skeletal Damage and Repair*. Champaign, IL: Human Kinetics Publishers, 2008.

....

Index

Page numbers in **boldface** are illustrations.

About the Author

L.H. Colligan writes about many to topics, from study skills to activity books and children's fiction and non-fiction on health and science topics. She lives in the Hudson Valley in New York. She keeps her muscles in shape by walking several miles a day, doing daily yoga, and enjoying healthy meals.